Horses Wear Shoes

and Other Questions About Horses

Jackie Gaff

KING*f*ISHER

NEW YORK

KINGFISHER
a Houghton Mifflin Company imprint
215 Park Avenue South
New York, New York 10003
www.houghtonmifflinbooks.com

First published in 2002

10 9 8 7 6 5 4 3 2 1

ITR/0502/TIM/RNB(RNB)115MA

LIBRARY OF CONGRESS CATALOGING-IN-PUBLICATION DATA
has been applied for.

ISBN 0-7534-5447-5

Series designer: David West Children's Books
Author: Jackie Gaff
Consultant: Jane Parker
Illustrations: Peter Dennis 18bl, 21br, 22, 23t,
    31b; James Field (SGA) 10-11, 13tr, 17tr,
    18-19t, 20, 21t, 23b, 24t, 25t, 26t, 27, 28-29,
    30, 31t; Lindsay Graham 6-7c, 9c, 12tl;
    Ian Jackson 4-5c, 6l, 12-13b, 14b, 16-17c, 26l;
    Nicki Palin 9tr, 9br, 24-25b; Eric Robson 7t;
    Richard Ward 8bl; Wendy Web 8tl;
    Peter Wilkes (SGA) all cartoons.

Printed in China

CONTENTS

4 What are a horse's good points?

5 Do horses have hands?

5 How can you tell
   a horse's age?

6 How can you tell
   if a horse is happy?

7 Do horses like company?

7 When is a horse a dam?

8 What is tack?

8 How do saddles
   help horses?

9 Why do riders
   wear helmets?

10 Which side of a
   horse do you mount?

10 How fast do horses move?

11 How do you dismount?

12 How high can horses jump?

12 Where do horses play games?

13 What is dressage?

14 Why do horses
    need grooming?

14 How often do horses need to eat?

15 Why do horses wear shoes?

16 How many kinds of horses are there?

16 Which are the smallest horses?

17 Which are the biggest horses?

18 Were horses around in dinosaur times?

18 When did people first tame horses?

19 Are there any wild horses left today?

20 When did horses chase lions?

20 Why is Bucephalus famous?

21 What kind of horse did knights ride?

22 Which horse had wings?

22 What was a centaur?

23 Whose horse had eight legs?

23 How do you catch a unicorn?

24 How did horses pull their weight?

24 When did stagecoaches begin running?

25 Why is the Pony Express famous?

26 What kind of work do horses do today?

27 Which horses do cowhands ride?

28 Which are the fastest horses?

28 What is a steeplechase?

29 Who sits in a sulky?

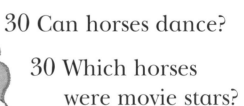

30 Can horses dance?

30 Which horses were movie stars?

31 What is a chukka?

31 Who rides a bucking bronco?

32 Index

What are a horse's good points?

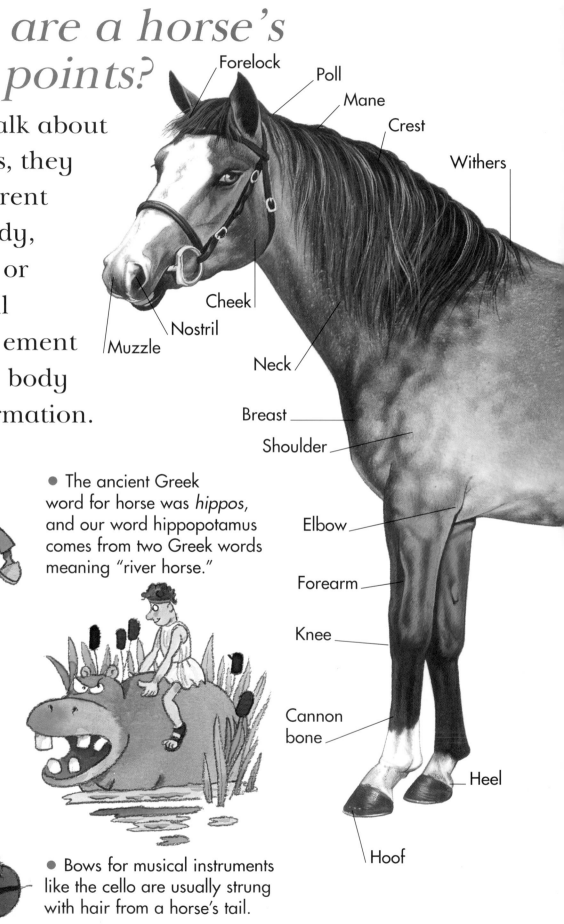

Forelock
Poll
Mane
Crest
Withers
Cheek
Nostril
Muzzle
Neck
Breast
Shoulder
Elbow
Forearm
Knee
Cannon bone
Heel
Hoof

When people talk about a horse's points, they mean the different parts of its body, such as its muzzle or its tail. The overall shape and arrangement of a horse's whole body is called its conformation.

• A female horse is called a mare, while a male horse is called a stallion.

• The ancient Greek word for horse was *hippos*, and our word hippopotamus comes from two Greek words meaning "river horse."

• Bows for musical instruments like the cello are usually strung with hair from a horse's tail.

Do horses have hands?

Not in the same way that you do! A horse's hands are the units used to measure its height from the ground to its withers— one hand equals about 4 in. (10cm).

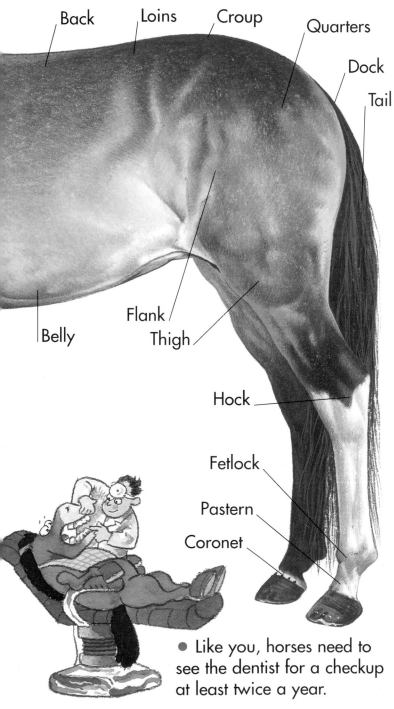

Back
Loins
Croup
Quarters
Dock
Tail
Belly
Flank
Thigh
Hock
Fetlock
Pastern
Coronet

- A pony is a small horse that measures 14.2 hands or less.

- Like you, horses need to see the dentist for a checkup at least twice a year.

How can you tell a horse's age?

Horses mainly eat grass, and munching away on this kind of tough plant food is very hard on teeth. Experts can get a good idea of a horse's age by looking at the way its teeth are wearing down as it gets older.

How can you tell if a horse is happy?

Although horses can't talk like we do, you can tell how a horse is feeling from its body language. For example, a happy horse will hold its head and tail up high.

Alert

Angry

Afraid

Content

● Zebras belong to the same animal family as horses, and so do donkeys and asses.

● Even a well-trained animal can have its bad days, so never walk or stand close to a horse's hind legs—you might get kicked.

Do horses like company?

They certainly do. Horses love hanging out in a herd—that's what we call a group of horses.

● Horses can sleep standing up. If they're in a herd, one horse will usually stay awake and watch out for danger while the others are dozing.

When is a horse a dam?

A mare is called a dam when she has babies. The babies are called foals, and a foal's father is its sire. Usually a mother horse gives birth to one foal at a time, after carrying it inside her for about one year.

● Horses are sometimes bred with donkeys—a mule has a donkey sire and a horse dam, while a hinny has a horse sire and a donkey dam. However, mules and hinnies can't have babies of their own.

What is tack?

Tack is the equipment a horse wears so that people can ride it. The main pieces are the bridle for its head and the saddle for its back.

Browband

Headpiece

Throatlash

Cheekpieces

Reins

Bit

Noseband

- Saddles were invented about 2,500 years ago. Before that people sat on a saddlecloth or rode bareback.

How do saddles help horses?

Saddles aren't just a comfy seat for the rider—they're also good for the horse. That's because the saddle helps put the rider's weight in the best position for the horse.

Seat

Girth

Pommel

Cantle

Stirrup

Saddle flap

- The girth is a strap that fits around the horse's belly to hold the saddle in place. It buckles up beneath the saddle flaps.

● There are many different saddles, including the Western ones used by cowhands. This saddle has an extra-high pommel called a horn, where the cowhand ties their lasso when roping cattle.

Horn

Why do riders wear helmets?

A rider's helmet is a lot like a motorcyclist's. It's designed to protect the head if a rider falls off and hits the ground.

● Cowhands protect their legs with seatless leather pants called chaps.

● Riding wasn't easy for women back in the days when they wore long skirts and only men wore pants. Women balanced on a sidesaddle, with their legs looped around big leather hooks on one side of the saddle.

Which side of a horse do you mount?

Most riders mount on the left—that means the horse is to your left when you're standing facing its tail. You put your left foot in the stirrup, spring off your right foot, and swing your right leg up and over the horse's back.

● Sit upright in the saddle with your legs against the horse's sides. Hold one rein in each hand.

How fast do horses move?

● Horses walk about as fast as you do, at about 4 miles per hour (6km/h).

We have only two ways of moving—walking and running. But horses have four—walking, trotting, cantering, and galloping. The fastest is the gallop, when horses can move along at well over 18.6 miles per hour (30km/h).

How do you dismount?

Once you can mount, you need to know how to get off again! Take both feet out of the stirrups, lean forward, swing your right foot over the horse's back, and jump gently down onto the ground.

● The custom of mounting a horse from the left probably began back in the days when men wore swords that hung down their left leg.

● A trotting horse does about 9 miles per hour (14km/h).

● A cantering horse can manage as much as 11 miles per hour (18km/h).

● Galloping, a horse can travel over 18.6 miles per hour (30km/h).

How high can horses jump?

● Walls are made of wooden bricks, so the horse isn't hurt if it knocks them down.

The highest fences in a top-level show jumping competition can be 6.5 feet (2m) or more—taller than the horse! The aim of riding a show jumping course is to get around it without knocking down any of the fences.

Where do horses play games?

A gymkhana is a riding competition with mounted games for single riders and teams. With games like the sack race and flag race, it's just like a relay race—on a horse!

● Winners and runners-up are awarded rosettes made from colored ribbons.

What is dressage?

Dressage is a special series of movements designed to show how well a horse and its rider work together. The movements include riding in a circle, a figure eight, and a curved shape called a serpentine.

FINISH

● Just about the toughest challenge for a horse and rider is eventing—a three-part competition covering dressage, show jumping, and racing around a cross-country course.

● One of the trickiest dressage moves is the pirouette, in which the horse canters in place in a circle.

Why do horses need grooming?

Grooming a horse helps keep its coat, skin, and feet clean and healthy. Most horses love being groomed, so it's also a great way for a horse and rider to become friends. Watch out—some horses are ticklish!

● Horses grow a thicker coat in the winter to help keep them warm. Sometimes this winter coat is clipped to keep the horse from sweating too much when it's ridden.

JUST A TRIM, PLEASE

How often do horses need to eat?

Horses need to be fed little and often because their stomachs are small for their size. They mainly eat grass or hay, which is dried grass.

● Horses love fruit and vegetables, especially apples and carrots.

Why do horses wear shoes?

Horseshoes stop hooves from being damaged by hard surfaces such as roads. The shoes are usually made of steel. The person who makes and fits them is called a blacksmith or farrier.

● Horseshoes have been used as good-luck charms for hundreds of years. Even today brides often carry a tiny silver horseshoe on their wedding day.

● Hooves are made of keratin, just like your fingernails. And like your nails, hooves grow all the time, so the farrier visits a stable every few weeks to trim the hooves and replace any worn shoes.

How many kinds of horses are there?

There are now more than 200 breeds of horses and ponies. Members of a breed share certain characteristics, such as color and height, and pass them on to their foals.

● A short, white marking on a horse's leg is called a sock, while a longer one is a stocking!

● There are special names for the different color combinations of a horse's coat, skin, mane, and tail.

1. Chestnut
2. Appaloosa
3. Fleabitten gray
4. Palomino
5. Black
6. Dapple gray
7. Piebald
8. Bay
9. Dun
10. Brown
11. Strawberry roan

Which are the smallest horses?

Ponies are, and the world's tiniest breed is the falabella. Small breeds are measured in centimeters—not hands—and falabellas grow to only about 75 centimeters (29.25 in.) high.

● Falabellas are too small to be ridden, but Shetland ponies grow a little taller and are the favorites of young riders.

Which are the biggest horses?

The giants of the horse world are the group of breeds known as draft horses. The giant of these heavy horse breeds is the shire. Shire horses grow to around 17 hands high and can weigh as much as one ton.

● The tallest-ever horse was a shire born in 1846. By the time it was six it measured 21.25 hands.

● The fringes of hair around a shire's feet are called feathers.

5

9

8

6

10

11

Were horses around in dinosaur times?

No. The earliest-known horse appeared on Earth about 50 million years ago, 15 million years after the dinosaurs died out. It's called Hyracotherium, and it was tiny—about the size of a fox.

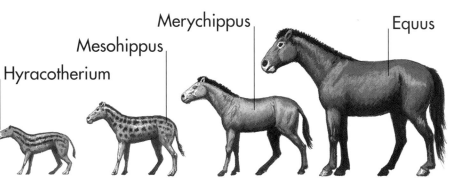

Hyracotherium   Mesohippus   Merychippus   Equus

• Equus, the kind of horse we know today, appeared about two million years ago.

• Cave paintings created more than 10,000 years ago show that long before the first horses were tamed, the people of prehistoric times hunted them, along with other wild animals, for their meat.

When did people first tame horses?

The first step in the taming of wild horses was to keep herds for their meat. This began happening around 6,000 years ago. Another few hundred years passed before people worked out how to train horses for riding.

• Hyracotherium had to avoid the flightless bird Diatryma— it was ten times the size of the tiny horse and had a big appetite!

• Feral (wild) horses are descended from tame horses that later escaped into the wild. Breeds include the mustangs in the U.S., the brumbies in Australia, and the camargue ponies in France.

Are there any wild horses left today?

There's only one breed of horse around now that's descended from the wild horses of prehistoric times. It is called Przewalski's horse after the Russian explorer who rediscovered it in Mongolia in the 1880s.

• Przewalski's horses died out in the wild in the 1960s. However, they had been bred in zoos, and they are now being set free again in Mongolia.

When did horses chase lions?

In ancient Egyptian times, around 3,000 years ago, lions roamed the Egyptian desert. Wealthy noblemen loved nothing more than a day spent hunting these ferocious wild animals, racing after them across the sands in a fast horse-drawn chariot.

Why is Bucephalus famous?

The black stallion Bucephalus was the warhorse of Alexander the Great, ruler of Macedonia and one of the greatest generals of all time. When Bucephalus died in 327 B.C., Alexander built a city and named it Bucephala in his honor.

● Bucephalus is said to have been so wild that no one could mount him—until the 12-year-old Alexander leapt on his back and rode him.

● Stories tell how ancient Greek warriors snuck inside the enemy city of Troy by hiding inside a huge wooden horse. When the Greek warriors opened the city gates after dark, their comrades poured in and burned Troy to the ground.

What kind of horse did knights ride?

In medieval times knights rode nimble, fast-moving horses into battle—these warhorses were about the same size as a modern show jumper. Knights rode a larger, heavier horse when they fought in mock battles called jousts.

Which horse had wings?

The ancient Greeks told marvelous stories about the adventures of a magical winged horse named Pegasus and his rider, Bellerophon. Their most famous adventure was killing the chimera—a three-headed, fire-breathing monster that was part-lion, part-goat, and part-snake.

What was a centaur?

The ancient Greeks believed in all kinds of strange creatures— for example, centaurs who were half-man, half-horse! Most centaurs were wild and dangerous. But Chiron was a wise, old centaur who was supposed to have taught legendary Greek heroes such as Jason.

Whose horse had eight legs?

The Vikings called the chief of their gods Odin. They believed he rode an eight-legged horse named Sleipnir, which could gallop across land, sea, and sky.

● The Valkyries were warrior women who rode across the sky to carry dead heroes to Odin's heavenly home, Valhalla.

How do you catch a unicorn?

In medieval times people loved stories about unicorns—magical horses with a long pointed horn on their forehead. People believed you could catch one by sending a maiden alone into the forest. When the unicorn came across the maiden, he would lay his head in her lap and fall asleep.

How did horses pull their weight?

Horses did almost all the heavy work before trains and motorcars were invented in the 1800s. They pulled cartloads of goods and carriageloads of people. They even hauled canal boats in Europe.

When did stagecoaches begin running?

Stagecoaches began carrying people between big towns and cities in the 1600s. Like trains and buses today, they were used by anyone who could afford the fare.

● Passengers trembled at the thought of being attacked by armed robbers called highwaymen. The most famous highwayman of all was Dick Turpin, who was hanged for his crimes in 1739.

• Shetland ponies worked underground in mine tunnels, hauling wagons loaded with coal and iron ore.

Why is the Pony Express famous?

Although it only operated for two years, from 1860–61, the Pony Express in the U.S. was world famous for its high-speed mail delivery service. Its riders carried letters and packages twice as fast as any stagecoach.

• Many Pony Express riders were lightweight teenagers because the less weight a horse has to carry, the faster it can gallop.

What kind of work do horses do today?

You're much taller than the rest of the crowd when you're mounted on a horse, and you can move faster than someone on foot. These are two good reasons for horses to work for city police forces throughout the world!

● Horses work while people are on vacation— pony trekking, for example, or carriage rides through city parks.

● The world's most famous mounted police officers are the Canadian mounties. These days, however, mounties only ride horses during special ceremonies.

● Women work as cowhands too. In Australia a jillaroo is a female apprentice, while a male apprentice is a jackeroo.

Which horses do cowhands ride?

Different horse breeds are ridden in different countries around the world. Some of the best four-legged workers are the camargue ponies of France, the Australian stock horses, the criollos of Argentina, and the quarter horses and mustangs of the U.S. and Mexico.

● Cowhand is an American term. These people are called guardians in France, gauchos in South America, stockmen in Australia, and vaqueros in Mexico.

Which are the fastest horses?

Racehorses are the kings of speed. A galloping racehorse can pound around a course with a jockey on its back at over 37 miles per hour (60km/h).

● Steeplechasing began in the 1750s in Ireland when two riders decided to test their horses' speeds by racing across country between two churches—chasing each other from steeple to steeple!

What is a steeplechase?

In a steeplechase horses have to jump fences, ditches, and other obstacles as they race around a course. A course without obstacles is a flat race.

Who sits in a sulky?

Jockeys do for a sport called harness racing. A sulky is a modern-day minichariot, which is attached to the horse by tack called a harness. The jockey perches on a seat over the sulky's wheels and guides the horse with extra-long reins.

● It doesn't matter on which day they were really born—all racehorses born in England have their official birthday on January 1.

Can horses dance?

Lipizzaners are the ballet dancers of the horse family, and the place to see them in action is the Spanish Riding School in Vienna, Austria. The school's beautiful white horses are world famous for their skillful grace, performing tricky dressage movements.

● This Lipizzaner stallion is performing a movement called the levade. In this the horse balances on its back legs and raises its front legs high up into the air.

● Roy Rogers and his palomino horse, Trigger, starred in many westerns during the 1940s and 1950s.

Which horses were movie stars?

Horses have starred in hundreds of movies. Where would westerns be without them, for example? Horses famous for their solo roles include Black Beauty and Champion the Wonder Horse, as well as the Lone Ranger's mount, Silver, and Roy Rogers', Trigger.